I0813997

THE STORY OF *Lamborghini*

First published in 2024 by Welbeck
An imprint of Headline Publishing Group Limited

4

Cataloguing in Publication Data is available from the British Library

ISBN 978-1-80279-851-7

Printed and bound in Italy

Headline's policy is to use papers that are natural, renewable and recyclable products and made from wood grown in well-managed forests and other controlled sources. The logging and manufacturing processes are expected to conform to the environmental regulations of the country of origin.

Editor: Conor Kilgallon
Design: Rebecca Hills
Production: Rachel Burgess

HEADLINE PUBLISHING GROUP LIMITED
A Hachette UK Company
Carmelite House
50 Victoria Embankment
London EC4Y 0DZ

The authorised representative in the EEA is Hachette Ireland,
8 Castlecourt Centre, Dublin 15, D15 XTP3, Ireland (email: info@hbgi.ie)

www.headline.co.uk
www.hachette.co.uk

THE STORY OF

Lamborghini

A TRIBUTE TO AUTOMOTIVE EXCELLENCE

STUART CODLING

Contents

The Sign of the Bull

Lamborghini

Go Your Own Way

"Lamborghini, you may be able to drive a tractor but you will never be able to handle a Ferrari properly."

Today, the arrival of an ambitious new sportscar manufacturer – launched by a respected businessman with the support of local government rather than vague promises of cash from venture capitalists – would no doubt be promulgated to the world via a slickly produced video hosted by a bellowing influencer. Lamborghini's launch possessed a subtlety that the brand and its cars would subsequently abandon. One of the first items of press coverage in Britain, for instance, came in the back pages of *Autocar* magazine in July 1963, where a rather dull monochrome image of a rolling chassis and engine appeared beside the similarly restrained headline "*Italian 3500cc GT from a new constructor*".

OPPOSITE: Ferruccio Lamborghini poses with an early version of his V12 engine and the 350 GTV prototype at the 1963 Turin show.

Contemporary sources might have documented Lamborghini's birth in drily factual tones but, over 60 years later, the company's history is draped appropriately in the seductive layers of myth essential to any supercar manufacturer in which the customer is buying into the story and image as much as the car. And what a story: a self-made man butting heads with a similarly pugnacious character – Enzo Ferrari – and resolving to beat him at his own trade.

Like any myth, only fragments of it may be true. But, as the newspaperman tells James Stewart's character in the classic film *The Man Who Shot Liberty Valance*, "*When the legend becomes fact, print the legend.*"

Believers in astrology hold that those born under the constellation of Taurus, the bull, are possessed of unusual strength and tenacity, and place great value on material pleasures. The sign itself is historically associated with the worship of bulls. Ferruccio Lamborghini was born in the Italian farming town of Renazzo on 28 April 1916, the week after Easter and a handful of days after the sign of the bull came into the ascendant. The youngest of five children, Lamborghini arrived into a Europe torn apart by war and civil disquiet, a cycle that would repeat during his lifetime.

Farming and artisan crafts have formed the backbone of the Emilia-Romagna region's economy since Roman times, when retiring legionaries were granted parcels of land as a reward for their services to the empire. There they worked the land or took up craft trades; as the decades passed, the region acquired a reputation for fine food, engineering and metalwork.

As a teenager, Lamborghini became more interested in the mechanics of the machines that worked the land than in cultivating the land itself. The modern Lamborghini myth holds that he built his own forge and machine shop on the family farm. It is widely claimed, though no documentation appears to exist, that he enrolled in a technical college – likely the Fratelli Taddia in nearby Bologna – to study engineering. But his date of birth placed him in the prime demographic to be compelled into military services when hostilities flared once more in 1939; a year later, aged 24, he was drafted into the Italian Air Force.

Ferruccio's mechanical skills came into play as a member of the ground crew servicing the aircraft fleet stationed on the Aegean island of Rhodes, a key hub with three airfields. Its strategic significance in this theatre of operations placed it in the line of fire from all sides: after Italy's surrender in 1943, Rhodes was attacked by both Allied and German forces during the Dodecanese campaign. Lamborghini spent several months as a prisoner of the Allies once hostilities ceased in 1945.

BELOW: Long before it adorned sportscars, the Lamborghini name featured on agricultural machinery.

BELOW: Ferruccio well understood the importance of getting the V12 engine right.

Freedom brought its own challenges. In common with the rest of his generation, Ferruccio came home to a country still suffering the privations of war – and, in Italy's case, the hangover from subjugation. Unemployment, poverty and starvation were rife in an economy that had fallen into inactivity after being repurposed for war: factories which had been converted to munitions manufacture lay idle, vehicles had been stripped or melted down to make engines of war. But here lay an opportunity for those with mechanical gifts and an entrepreneurial mindset.

Italy's bread basket needed to produce again. Ferruccio, according to the company's origin myth, built his parents a new tractor out of scavenged components and then, while on honeymoon, came across a British army detachment disposing

of Italian military equipment. Whether this is true or not, Lamborghini started his first business repurposing ex-military vehicles for agricultural use or raiding them for spare parts to maintain existing farm machinery. The work was tough, but profitable; and, once the available stock of army-surplus hardware began to run low, he established Lamborghini Tractori SpA to manufacture complete new vehicles – including engines. Success enabled Ferruccio to employ more staff and step back from the hands-on work, though he continued to modify road cars, souping up several 569cc Fiat Topolinos for himself and other acquaintances. With one, bored and stroked to 750cc, he entered the 1948 Mille Miglia road race; the records enshrine him as a plain DNF – Did Not Finish – but the story behind the acronym is typically flamboyant.

"*I finished my Mille Miglia in an osteria* [pub]," he said, "*which I entered by driving through the wall.*"

Whether you believe it or not, this plausibly accounts for Lamborghini's future aversion to motor racing. He became a wealthy man in the 1950s as his tractor company prospered and he established a second business building and maintaining air-conditioning systems, a wildly popular growth industry that had sprung up in the USA. Like any new technology manufactured at scale it was inclined to be temperamental, and Lamborghini was careful to ensure his aftersales service was among the best in the field, encouraging repeat business.

When Lamborghini began to reward himself for his success by acquiring luxury cars, he was therefore on a collision course with the notoriously prickly Enzo Ferrari. If, once again, the myth is to be believed.

Ferruccio certainly delighted in repeating the legend often enough to establish it as fact, though certain details would often shift to suit the occasion. He said the following in a 1991 interview with *Thoroughbred & Classic Cars* magazine:

OPPOSITE: In 1968, for the third year in a row, Lamborghini turned heads on the motor show circuit – this time with the launch of the dramatic Espada.

"After I got my first Ferrari, my other six cars – Alfa Romeo, Lancia, Mercedes, Maserati, Jaguar – were always left in the garage. In 1958 I went to Maranello for the first time to buy a 250GT coupé, the two-seater by Pininfarina. After that I had one, maybe two, 250GT Berlinettas, the short-wheelbase car from Scaglietti. I did like that one very much. It was ahead of its time, had a perfect balance and a strong engine. Finally, I bought a 250GT 2+2, which was a four-seater by Pininfarina. That engine was very strong too and it went very well.

"All my Ferraris had clutch problems. When you drove normally, everything was fine. But when you were going hard, the clutch would slip under acceleration; it just wasn't up to the job. I went to Maranello regularly to have a clutch rebuilt or renewed, and every time, the car was taken away for several hours and I was not allowed to watch them repairing it. The problem with the clutch was never cured, so I decided to talk to Enzo Ferrari. I had to wait for him a very long time. 'Ferrari, your cars are rubbish!' I complained. Il Commendatore was furious. 'Lamborghini, you may be able to drive a tractor but you will never be able to handle a Ferrari properly.' This was the point when I finally decided to make a perfect car."

Subsequent accounts from Lamborghini's early employees have applied somewhat unwanted layers of reality to this story. Ubaldo Sgarzi, sales manager and the man who did so much to keep the company alive during the 1970s, would later say Ferruccio's 250 GT 2+2 merely had faulty spark plugs and poorly set up carburettors.

Both test driver/engineer Bob Wallace and his successor, Valentino Balboni, have suggested that comparing what Ferrari was charging for a new clutch with what Lamborghini billed customers for tractor clutches set Ferruccio to thinking what profit could be made from building grand touring cars. He was too astute to enter such a potentially risky start-up

DI

BELOW: Local government concessions enabled Lamborghini to build an impressive new factory.

business based on a clash of egos alone, but he recognized the opportunity to turn a profit if the product hit the mark.

"In the past I have bought some of the most expensive Gran Turismo cars," he explained in a 1964 interview with *Sporting Motorist* magazine.

"And in each of these magnificent cars I have found some faults. Too hot. Or uncomfortable. Or not sufficiently fast. Or not perfectly finished. Now I want to make a GT car without faults. Not a technical bomb. Very normal. But a perfect car."

Ferruccio enjoyed telling interviewers how he and his mechanics improved his Ferrari themselves in the Lamborghini tractor workshop, fitting a larger aftermarket Borg & Beck clutch and adding new twin-camshaft cylinder heads and horizontally mounted carburettors. With equal relish he would describe waiting for Ferrari factory test drivers outside Modena and then racing them up the A1 autostrada.

Lamborghini would receive no pushback against his plans from local authorities. The state of the economy was such that the Communist party held the majority in regional government, signing off on his plans for a new factory and granting an interest-free loan to build it provided he employed local workers – and provided they were members of the sheet metal workers' union. While this limited Ferruccio's own financial risk, the deal for inexpensive labour left his young company vulnerable to union caprice for years to come.

In a corner of the tractor factory, the chassis of the first prototype came together through the energy of an ambitious team of young engineers: Giampaolo Dallara, who had joined Ferrari immediately after graduating from the Milan Technical Institute at the age of 24, became technical director, assisted by recent University of Bologna graduate Paolo Stanzani. Giotto Bizzarrini, one of the architects of the iconic Ferrari 250 GTO, took on a freelance engagement as a consultant. Design and production of the bodywork was to be outsourced, as was customary at the time in low-volume car manufacture: in the early days of Ferrari the company simply produced rolling chassis with engines and transmissions which were clothed in bespoke shells by traditional coachbuilders. Soulless production lines which stamped out homogenous tin boxes were for the likes of Ford.

The project was beset with difficulties from the outset. As we will explore in the following chapter, the headstrong, individualistic Bizzarrini was paid based on the final power output of the 3.5-litre V12 engine. The initial result was not to Ferruccio's liking. Nor would it fit in the prototype car Lamborghini unveiled to the public at the 1963 Turin motor show. Ferruccio had the front end ballasted with tiles and the bonnet locked; if any sales prospects asked to look inside, Lamborghini would gesture at one of his employees and say, "*See*

RIGHT: From the earliest models, such as the 350 GT pictured here, Lamborghini aimed for a luxurious interior feel with plenty of leather.

that idiot? He's lost the keys." The engine was displayed separately to the rest of the car.

The 350 GTV prototype's bodywork design was credited to Franco Scaglione, working to a tight brief from Ferruccio, and the show car was built by the newly established Carrozzeria Sargiotto. But Lamborghini's plans had already changed by the time the car made its public debut: he was dissatisfied with the dated styling, as well as the raciness of Bizzarrini's tube frame chassis and the indifferent build quality of the shell.

Dallara and Stanzani took over onward development as Bizzarrini moved on to other freelance projects. Their new chassis design, based on square sections, was more suited to scale production. Carrozzeria Touring of Milan, early Ferrari collaborators and inventors of the patented Superleggera (super-light) construction technique, reworked Scaglione's design into a simpler and more classically elegant shape. Dallara also revised the engine for a more relaxed power delivery.

Unveiled at the 1964 Geneva show, the 350 GT received favourable press but didn't really manage to engage with potential customers at all: Lamborghini took just 13 orders all year. Ferruccio, keen to offer a larger and more powerful car to compete with Ferrari's 275, abandoned plans to introduce a smaller-engined model and went the other way, asking Dallara to increase the swept volume of the V12 to four litres. He hired Wallace, an aspiring racing driver from New Zealand who had worked as a mechanic for the Scuderia Serenissima racing organization, to improve the driving dynamics of Lamborghini's cars.

BELOW: Although reviews of the 350 GT were positive, sales proved disappointing.

OVERLEAF: Restyled and boasting a larger engine, plus room for two (small) rear passengers, the 400 GT was a step up from the 350 GT.

ABOVE: The bold Marzal show car prefaced the arrival of the Espada.

Despite financial issues, Touring were able to handle production demands for the new 400 GT model, although Zagato pitched for business with a pair of concept cars based on that car's running gear. The definitive 400 GT 2+2 was launched in 1966, featuring a Lamborghini-made gearbox and differential in place of the off-the-shelf ZF components used in earlier cars, as well as a reshaped chassis to accommodate a pair of rear seats in place of the original – and curious – sideways-mounted single rear seat. When Touring went bust, production shifted

to Carrozzeria Marazzi, a new company whose workforce was boosted by the recruitment of ex-Touring personnel.

While accomplished enough in their own way, these first Lamborghinis were relaxed grand tourers – the kind of car Ferruccio and other middle-aged men of means would choose to reward themselves for their success. They sold steadily but not in exciting numbers. Realizing the range needed to be expanded, Ferruccio signed off on the attention-grabbing Marzal concept vehicle and Miura supercar, followed

BELOW: It may seem unfamiliar now, but the Espada was Lamborghini's biggest seller of the 1970s across three model generations.

OPPOSITE: Relaunched as the Islero with pop-up headlights and a new interior, the GT model still failed to excite buyers.

eventually by a first attempt at a higher volume model, named the Urraco.

In 1968 Mario Marazzi rebodied the 400 GT – reputedly, his pen very much guided by Ferruccio – with more interior space, a larger glasshouse and pop-up headlights. The 'new' car was badged as the Islero, named after a famous fighting bull, and it sold in modest quantities – 125 – until the updated Islero S model was released a year later. Although Ferruccio adopted one as his daily driver, the Islero was never as successful as the more adventurous Espada, which was launched alongside it at the 1968 Geneva motor show. Designed by Miura stylist Marcello Gandini and based on styling themes established on the Marzal, it would become Lamborghini's biggest-selling model in the first two decades of the company's existence. The bull was up and running.

Paid by the Horse

Inside the Engine Room

"I'll make it bigger and more powerful..."

The genesis of Lamborghini's astoundingly long-lived V12 engine – with development it powered the company's flagship cars for nearly 40 years – is as wreathed in myth as the origin story of Lamborghini itself. Popular legend has it that freelance engineer Giotto Bizzarrini was paid per unit of horsepower, an incentive which drove him to deliver an unusably peaky engine which would only have been useful in a racing car.

The truth is somewhat more nuanced. Lamborghini employees at the time recall that Ferruccio had not decided – or at least had not made it clear – what character the V12 should have. Bizzarrini's version of events was that he showed Ferruccio drawings of a 1.5-litre quad-cam V12 Formula 1 engine he had designed and was told to build a 3-litre version that would match Ferrari's equivalent road unit for power. "*I'll make it bigger and more powerful,*" Bizzarrini claimed he replied, agreeing to a fixed fee with a bonus for every unit of horsepower over 300 he could squeeze from it.

OPPOSITE: Everything about the Miura was dramatic, right down to the black 'eyelashes' framing the pop-up headlamps.

RIGHT: The Miura's chassis, with the V12 engine mounted transversely behind the cabin, was a rarity outside the world of motor racing.

Born in 1926, Bizzarrini graduated in mechanical engineering at the University of Pisa and spent four years in the mid-1950s working for Alfa Romeo on chassis development before joining Ferrari in 1957, initially as a test driver. At Maranello he quickly made a name for himself. Independent and iconoclastic, he led the work to cure the handling balance and aerodynamic issues plaguing Ferrari's new 250 GT SWB, a project eventually finished by Mauro Forghieri after Bizzarrini and a group of other senior staff quit *en masse* in November 1961.

The most outward nod to competition with the cars Ferrari was making was the presence of twin cams per cylinder bank rather than single ones, though the choice of alloy material for the crankcase was also rare in road cars. Initially displacing 3465cc, the 60-degree V12 was laden with race-inspired features including dry-sump lubrication and down-draught carburettors. Bizzarrini claimed 370bhp at 9,500rpm and insisted that with the right fuelling system it could be persuaded to reach 400bhp.

It ultimately fell to Dallara to make the engine less overtly racy, converting it from dry-sump to wet-sump lubrication and swapping out the vertical Weber carburettors for their less costly side-draught equivalents. A lower compression ratio and less edgy valve timing made it less peaky, although claimed maximum power was still reasonable: 270bhp at 6,500rpm in the first 350 GT models. The subsequent increase in displacement to 4 litres, achieved by increasing the cylinder bore from 77mm to 82mm, brought peak power to 320bhp at 6,500rpm while broadening the torque curve for a more relaxed delivery.

Another left-field theory about the Lamborghini V12's journey from draughtpaper to engine bay was put forward in the 1980s by motoring journalist L. J. K. Setright, a self-taught engineer. He claimed to have been told by a credible source that Bizzarrini's design was essentially discarded and a new V12 commissioned in secret from Honda. Described by no less an eminence than Bob Wallace as 'crap', the proposition has little evidence to support it bar some shared details between the Lamborghini engine and Honda's 1.5-litre V12, which raced in Formula 1 in 1965.

Dallara was also working on a pet project which would pave the way for the model that would truly put Lamborghini on the map. A persistent legend has it that the Miura was developed without Ferruccio's knowledge, and with the implicit aim of trying to steer him towards building a high-performance car rather than proceed with stately grand tourers. Certainly, according to the principals, the first brainstorming sessions took place outside office hours. But Dallara is on record as saying Ferruccio okayed the acquisition of a Mini to hack about into a rolling proof-of-concept chassis.

"I had nothing else to do on a Saturday or a Sunday anyway, and had a whole factory to play around with," wrote Dallara in

ABOVE: It might look unsophisticated to modern eyes but, at the 1965 Turin show, Lamborghini's mid-engined rolling chassis generated huge excitement.

his autobiography *It's A Beautiful Story*:

"Let's build a lighter car to show it could be done. Have some sort of a mobile test bed for new ideas or trying something different, that sort of thing.

"He [Ferruccio] *told me, 'You can do whatever the hell you want to do as long as it doesn't interfere with your daily job.' You get up and start testing at five in the morning, and drive and play around until three in the afternoon, and then go and play around trying to build something. Well, I didn't have anything better to do, and I've always enjoyed cars and still do. But as far as any serious effort to build a race car, no, that's something that writers and journalists and people in the past just sort of invented."*

By the mid-1960s, mid-engined cars were common in motor racing – essential in Formula 1 and rapidly becoming so in other categories. When Lamborghini displayed a rolling chassis at the 1965 Turin show with the V12 mounted transversely behind the driver, the only road cars sharing this configuration were rareties: the De Tomaso Vallelunga, the ATS 2500GT and the René

BELOW: Bertone won the bid to design and build the bodywork for the Miura.

Bonnet Djet. On the racetrack, Ford's mid-engined GT40 was beginning to win the battle against Ferrari, a company which came to the concept only grudgingly (Enzo Ferrari famously opined that the horse should pull the cart rather than pushing it, and was resistant to changing that viewpoint). The show chassis, badged P400, clearly followed racing practice in that it was based around a central 'tub' with three longitudinal box-section members (drilled to reduce weight) connected by the floor and by bulkheads at each end. Further box sections extended fore and aft to act as engine and suspension mounting points.

As with the Mini dissected by Dallara for his proof of concept, the engine block was now cast in one piece with the transmission and differential, sharing the same oil sump, to achieve a compact form factor and sit ahead of the rear wheels. If Ferruccio had, as is said, agreed to exhibit the chassis merely

as a stunt to trumpet his company's engineering excellence, he came away from the show with a fistful of provisional orders for a car he had yet to build – and a queue of coachbuilders eager to provide a bodyshell design and final assembly service. The last one to bid, nervously, was Nuccio Bertone – on the last day of the show.

Since Carrozzeria Touring was lurching towards insolvency at this point, Lamborghini was open to alternatives and Bertone received the commission. New recruit Marcello Gandini worked closely with Dallara to create a new mid-engined vehicle which would define a new genre: the supercar. According to Paolo Stanzani's account, he and Dallara were very specific that it should be a race car for the road, citing the GT40 as the state of the mid-engined art. On Christmas Eve 1965 Stanzani and Dallara presented Gandini's styling proposal to Ferruccio, whose response (so they say) was: "*Make it.*"

BELOW: Despite a clamshell rear deck design, access to the engine was limited.

ABOVE: Later Miura SV models can be distinguished by the absence of eyelashes around the headlamps.

By the following March, a prototype bodyshell was ready to sit on the chassis for launch at the Geneva motor show, rendered even more eye-catching by the choice of colour: "*Poised somewhere between yellow and orange*" as Setright put it. Now officially christened the Miura P400 – after Eduardo Miura, the breeder whose fighting bulls inspired Lamborghini's logo – the new car caused a sensation. The GT40 had taken its name from its aggressively low stance, just 40 inches (1m) from ground level to roof panels, and the Miura was just 1.5 inches (3.8cm) taller. Shell-like one-piece nose and tail panels aimed to demonstrate the continued supremacy of Italian artisan construction. They also offered unusually easy access to the engine bay and luggage compartment, provided the owner or mechanic had the muscle to open them.

The interior was incomplete and would remain a work-in-progress throughout the Miura's life. Before the official unveiling, Ferruccio jotted down on paper how many he expected to sell that year, challenging the principals of the project to do the same. He wrote 20. Nuccio Bertone (perhaps with a view to how many bodyshells his company could realistically make) thought 5, chief salesman Ubaldo Sgarzi put down 50, while the ever-bullish Dallara imagined Lamborghini could build and sell 100.

It took until the end of the following year to hit Dallara's figure. Development and infrastructure snags delayed serial production until the second half of 1966, as the 300-strong staff at the new Sant'Agata factory got to grips with the process. Rather than building a rolling chassis which was then sent to the coachbuilder for finishing – the traditional model, as followed by Ferrari until the late 1960s – Lamborghini had Bertone send the painted shells to Sant'Agata for the final fit. Quality was initially sub-par and many early Miura owners had their interiors re-trimmed by other coachbuilders. The scattershot ergonomics

BELOW: Build quality was occasionally inexact – the large gaps between panels wouldn't be tolerated by modern supercar buyers.

ABOVE: Though shapely and beautiful, the Miura was aerodynamically poor and prone to front-end 'lift'.

were outside the influence of these seasoned professionals, though: only the speedometer and rev counter sat directly ahead of the driver, and were partly blocked by the steering wheel, while dials indicating parameters such as fuel level and oil pressure sat with no obvious hierarchy in a central panel. Deploying the headlights required the driver to operate two separate switches, one in the roof panel and one by the gearlever.

Externally, the production Miuras differed from the prototype only in details, such as the rear screen (changed from wraparound plexiglass to a black slatted arrangement) and headlamp 'eyelashes' (which popped up with the lights

on the show car). As with the general fit and finish, the driving dynamics of the first examples provided ample evidence of a product still in beta. "*Our customers were the test drivers,*" Dallara would later say, since Wallace was somewhat overstretched by having to combine general model development with quality assurance on the initial cars.

Some of the teething troubles, such as the overly heavy steering and the tendency of poorly set-up carburettors to cause flash fires, were straightforward to fix. Less so was the baked-in aerodynamic lift at high speeds caused by the long curve of the bonnet.

"Anyone who has achieved a true 170mph in a Miura can tell you that the effect experienced is that of a jet plane on a runway (complete with imminent take-off!)," wrote marque enthusiast Joe Sackey in *The Lamborghini Miura Bible*, *"and the relationship between man, machine and God's green earth at that speed is a fragile one, compressed time-travel if you like, only to be undertaken by those brave souls who dare. You haven't lived until you've tried it... some say."*

While the bodyshell might have been aerodynamically sub-optimal, it was undoubtedly beautiful – and would become a source of controversy many years later as two of the twentieth century's most eminent automotive stylists tussled for credit over its authorship. Giorgetto Giugiaro, whose CV encompasses classics such as the Lotus Esprit, Volkswagen Golf, BMW M1, Maserati Ghibli and Alfa Romeo Giulia GT, worked at Bertone until 1965. In the mid-1990s he began to claim in a series of interviews that Gandini merely finished off the details of initial sketches he had left behind. Later on, Giugiaro engaged reverse gear on this claim.

In 1968 Lamborghini released the revised Miura P400S, with a stiffer chassis and revised transmission and rear suspension. While this did nothing for the aerodynamic lift issues, it improved mechanical refinement and sweetened the handling response. Larger intake manifolds and more aggressive camshaft profiles elevated the V12's claimed power to 370bhp.

At the Brussels motor show that year, the company demonstrated an open-top Miura. Resplendent in metallic powder blue with a white leather interior, this roadster model subtly defied convention: rather than simply decapitate the car and replace the metal with folding fabric, Lamborghini removed only the upper section of the roof. Here function dictated form, since the chassis had to be augmented for safety and to reduce flex caused by the loss of the roof panel. Gandini cleverly integrated the rollover bar into a flying buttress structure and removed the slatted black rear screen to expose the engine, making it a design feature.

The official company history claims that Ferruccio refused to build a production model. In truth Bertone insisted on a minimum of 50 orders before committing to production and, despite great interest at the show, Lamborghini did not pass this threshold. The show car then enjoyed an interesting second life as a promotional tool for the International Lead Zinc Research Organization, which stripped it and galvanised the bodyshell to demonstrate the corrosion-resistance of coated metals. While Lamborghini never offered a roadster model for sale to the public, a number of owners have subsequently committed the ultimate sacrilege of having their Miuras converted.

Dallara also took his leave that year, moving to De Tomaso to design a Formula 1 car. It is widely believed that Ferruccio's refusal to countenance a racing programme (*see* Chapter 5) played a part in his decision to move. Paolo Stanzani, who took

BELOW: The company's Polo Storico division now offers complete new body panels for restoration projects.

OVERLEAF: Conceptually the low, wide, mid-engined Miura had much in common with Ford's Le Mans-winning GT40.

ABOVE: Dynamically the Miura SV model was a great improvement over the original.

over as technical director, has claimed that Ferruccio wanted to step back and hand day-to-day management of the company to him rather than Dallara, prompting Giampaolo to quit in a temper. Dallara's account is that he saw the troubles which would result in the company's sale coming.

The eminent engineer might have required a crystal ball to reach this verdict. It was not until 1969 that Lamborghini encountered the first major bumps in the road, as industrial unrest rippled across Italy and a series of strikes called by the Communist-controlled unions brought work at Sant'Agata to a halt. To begin with this had little effect on car development, as Stanzani oversaw work on new models as well as the final iteration of the Miura, and Wallace quietly fettled his Miura race car outside office hours. And sales, at least of the flagship car, were going well: Frank Sinatra arrived unannounced one day, was given an impromptu tour of the factory by

Ubaldo Sgarzi, and left having placed an order for a P400S in metallic orange with boarskin leather trim and orange shagpile carpeting.

Launched at the Geneva show in 1971, the 400SV was the definitive Miura. Outwardly different only through the wider rear track and absence of 'eyelashes', the SV represented another significant step in performance and refinement. Revised suspension front and rear added further finesse to the Miura's dynamics, as did the limited-slip differential. New three-barrel carburettors and valve timing, as well as a different combustion chamber design, delivered a claimed 15bhp boost. Lamborghini also took the opportunity to split the oil reservoirs for the engine and gearbox, a measure which improved peace-of-mind rather than performance.

Was this to be the ultimate Lamborghini? No. 'Project 112' was already on the drawing board.

Countach!

An Icon is Born

"A high-speed, low-drag container for two lucky people."

Beautiful and beguiling as the Miura was, it was freighted with hardwired shortcomings – ones which Paolo Stanzani and assistant Massimo Parenti, along with test driver/engineer Bob Wallace, recognized that despite their best efforts could not be resolved without beginning again from a clean sheet. Ferruccio Lamborghini shared their concerns about the Miura's twitchy on-the-limit demeanour, recalcitrant gear change, the heat and noise of a V12's reciprocating parts just a few inches away from the driver's ears, and the front end's propensity to try to achieve take-off at high speed.

Ferruccio also had wider concerns about his model range. The De Tomaso Mangusta, Maserati Bora and Ferrari 365 GTB/4 had emerged as rivals to the Miura. And, while his supercar was achieving reasonable sales figures, Ferruccio's other offerings were failing to interest their respective demographics. His beloved grand tourers had fallen particularly flat; the 350GT begat the 400GT begat the Islero to widespread indifference, thanks in part to the outdated method of manufacture and hit-and-miss quality of

OPPOSITE: Cooling the engine was one of the biggest challenges as Lamborghini gradually expanded the V12's swept volume to 5.2 litres.

ABOVE: A largely complete Countach bodyshell arrives at the factory to be mated to the mechanicals.

Carrozzeria Materazzi's work. A final throw of the dice – the Jarama, named after a breed of fighting bulls rather than the dreary racetrack near Madrid – shared many mechanicals and some styling features with the more successful Espada, but still proved a flop. The Urraco, an attempt to colonize a market segment dominated by Porsche's 911 with Ferrari's Dino 246 GT as the challenger, received good reviews but was delayed by persistent problems with its transmission and new V8 engine. Permeating this scenario like a poisonous miasma, ongoing industrial unrest sapped both cash flow and Ferruccio's will, as production lagged and orders were cancelled.

'Project 112' began to come together in 1970, before the Urraco's first public appearance at the Turin motor show. At this point confidence was high that the new mid-market sportscar would be a success, and the Miura's replacement could therefore be more rarefied; Ferruccio even planned to offer it only to existing customers personally approved by himself. As such, money – both in terms of the development budget and the final asking price – could be less of an object. Project 112 would be neither a GT nor a race car. Stanzani could create his own genre – so long as the finished product hit its performance benchmarks.

Some might view the move to a spaceframe chassis as a retrograde step, but this was a logical response to the need for greater overall stiffness given that the engine was to be rotated and moved further forwards within the structure. A conventional north-south location for the engine opened the possibilities for better cooling architecture and improved exhaust routing, with potential power benefits. The key challenge was the inherent length of a V12: how to locate it far enough forwards to avoid the Miura's penchant for snap oversteer while still maintaining a polite distance from the driver? Stanzani addressed this by mounting the gearbox and clutch at the front of the engine with the differential at the rear, connected by a shaft running through a sealed tunnel within the sump. Although it added some weight, and raised the centre of gravity relative to a more conventional layout, it offset this by locating more mass within the wheelbase. It also offered a shorter and more direct linkage for the gear-selector mechanism, eliminating another Miura flaw.

The new layout, and the expansion of the engine to 5 litres by increasing both bore and stroke, led to Project 112 being renamed LP500 (LP for *Longitudinale Posteriore*, signifying the V12's alignment and location). Soon it would become *Countach*, a Piedmontese vernacular exclamation with no exact translation in English, usually uttered by young men appreciating the sight of an attractive woman. (These were the 1970s…). Quite who said it first when they witnessed Marcello Gandini's dynamic

OPPOSITE: Before it acquired the Countach name, the prototype appeared as the LP500 at the 1971 Geneva Show. It was later destroyed in crash testing, though Lamborghini's Polo Storico department recreated it for the 50th anniversary in 2021.

wedge-shaped design for the first time is impossible to say for certain. Differing accounts attribute it to Ferruccio Lamborghini and Nuccio Bertone, but plenty of others were moved to utter the word when covers came off the LP500 prototype at Geneva in 1971. This was not Gandini's first wedge – his Lancia Stratos Zero concept with a vast, hinged windscreen had wowed Turin show-goers six months earlier – but it still caused a stir. Gandini explained that his design began with a single sweeping line from nose to tail and every other aspect of the car's stance, proportions and detailing proceeded from there. To make the doors fulfil their function within the desired shapes, Gandini dictated that they hinge forwards and upwards like scissors.

Ultimately, some engineering features – such as the extensive use of magnesium in the suspension and steering, the aircraft-style yoke instead of a steering wheel, and the digital instruments – did not make it through to production. The spaceframe chassis design was also revised with additional tubing in place of sheet steel. Practicality also had to be accommodated, with a periscope-style rear viewing mirror arrangement on early models, and secondary windows which could actually open so the driver did not have to disembark to pay tolls on the Autostrada.

The LP500's journey to becoming the Countach would, like the Urraco's arrival on the market, suffer excruciating delays. If the Lamborghini stand at Geneva in 1971 – featuring the LP500, Jarama, new Series II Espada and Urraco – suggested a company continuing to grow aggressively, this was far from the case. A global energy crisis was brewing, threatening the marketability of high-performance cars, and the global economy was in slowdown, affecting this and Ferruccio's other businesses.

Also, it was a strategic mistake to flag up two new cars at the same time: customers were holding back from buying the established models. There was not enough money in the development pot to advance the Urraco and Countach to

production readiness quickly, even if Lamborghini had sufficient engineering resources to accomplish the task. The development team was stretched too thin.

The solution was to prioritize. The 5-litre version of the V12 persistently overheated so, since the Urraco's problematic V8 was already hogging resource, Stanzani reverted to the 4-litre. Once it was possible to drive the Countach prototype for more than a few miles without boiling the engine, the car proved to be far more skittish at the rear than expected as speeds built while travelling in a straight line. In an era before the widespread use of wind tunnels for research into road and race car aerodynamics, Wallace, Stanzani and Parenti glued wool tufts to the prototype's shell and fired off motor-drive shots of it at speed from a camera mounted to a chase car. This revealed the Countach was generating too much downforce at the front,

ABOVE: The Countach was also dramatic on the inside, if ergonomically challenging.

OPPOSITE: When cooling proved problematic, the first solution was to revert to the 4-litre version of the V12 and add NACA ducts and boxy scoops to the Countach's flanks.

hence the rear-end liveliness while pressing on, and not enough cooling air was reaching the radiators from the louvres on the car's shoulders.

Lamborghini's tractor business also faced headwinds. The company had made major investments to fufil a large order from Bolivia, but the country's socialist government was subsequently toppled in a coup d'etat. Another substantial order was cancelled.

Most companies would respond to these scenarios by, however grudgingly, reducing production and laying off staff. The Communist-controlled trade unions refused to accommodate such necessary big-picture thinking, forcing Ferruccio to dip into his own pockets to keep churning out tractors and cars destined to remain unsold. To ensure a comfortable retirement he held on to his air conditioning and pneumatic valve businesses, sold the tractor company to his main rival, and reached a deal with Swiss

ABOVE: Dramatic 'scissor' doors made it through to production. Tyre availability dictated a maximum 14-inch rear-wheel size on early models.

sportscar enthusiast Georges-Henri Rossetti to acquire a 51 per cent stake in the car manufacturer for a reported $600,000.

In May 1972 Stanzani and Wallace drove the Countach prototype to Sicily and back to watch the Targa Florio road race. It survived the journey and, upon its successful return to Sant-Agata, Ferruccio and Rossetti officially sanctioned production. It would be another two years before the LP400

Countach was ready for the market, by which time it had grown a pair of NACA ducts and boxy air intakes on each side for the sake of engine cooling. Of greater import was the fact that the company founder had retired to his Umbrian estate after selling his remaining 49 per cent stake to another Swiss, René Leimer, for $400,000. The decline in relative value of the stock was reflective of market conditions: conflict in the Middle East had

OPPOSITE: Giampaolo Dallara returned to Lamborghini as a consultant in 1976, overseeing important revisions that would result in the much-improved LP400 S model.

caused a spike in oil prices and sent already teetering economies worldwide into recession. Performance cars were out of fashion, and not just as a factor of increased costs at the pump; several countries, including Italy, imposed additional sales taxes on cars with engines displacing more than 2 litres.

As such the LP400 Countach was released into a very different atmosphere to the one which had greeted the LP500 three years earlier. What was once outlandishly alluring was now deemed borderline irrelevant. Contemporary road-testers were impressed by its performance, less so by its poise and roadholding. It had been developed on experimental Pirelli tyres which the company never put on sale, forcing Lamborghini to fit Michelin XWXs, then the largest tyres available in terms of width; but they were also high-profile, enforcing a maximum wheel size of 14 inches.

While Leimer and Rossetti were enthusiastic about cars, they had been born into wealth – Rossetti was the scion of a watchmaking dynasty – and lacked understanding of the ways of working folk. Neither was adequately equipped to handle febrile industrial relations or the effects of global recession on the sportscar market. The Urraco never achieved the originally anticipated sales volumes despite very favourable reviews in the motoring press; and the Countach proved too slow to make, since the spaceframe was outsourced and too many minor components had to be hand-crafted in-house. It is ironic that even in this climate Lamborghini proved unable to satisfy demand for its halo car, making just 23 in 1974. With the company in retrenchment, it was likely there would be no investment in development of new or existing cars, so both Stanzani and Wallace departed in 1975.

The arrival of new Europe-wide type-approval regulations in 1978, imposing tougher and more extensive crash-testing procedures, demanded action and signified the end for the Urraco and Espada models. Giampaolo Dallara returned on

countach

BELOW: From the LP400 S model onwards the Countach gained a rear wing, wheel arch extensions and bigger tyres, as the engine expanded.

ABOVE: The original design was so futuristic that it remained iconic over a decade later, in the 1980s, an era when anything else from the 1970s was considered passé at best.

a consultancy basis in 1976, reworking the Urraco into what would become the Silhouette and overseeing an important redevelopment of the Countach. Pirelli's new low-profile P7 tyres enabled Dallara to completely rework the suspension geometry, fit 15-inch wheels at the rear, and install larger brake rotors, all of which contributed to a more confidence-inspiring drive. The LP400S was launched in 1978 – shortly before failed projects instigated by Leimer and Rossetti left Lamborghini bankrupt.

Thanks to a sympathetic administrator (*see* Chapter 4), production of the Countach continued during this period and onward through several of Lamborghini's subsequent custodians. The eminent engineer Giulio Alfieri, architect of many iconic road and racing Maseratis, produced the next iteration. In fitting a large rear wing to improve stability, along with the necessary bodywork extensions to accommodate the larger wheels and tyres, Dallara had exacerbated drag on a car that in reality was already less slippery than it looked to the naked eye. To improve performance, Alfieri and new recruit Luigi Marmiroli fell back on the expedient of enlarging the engine to 4.8 litres. Though offset slightly by a modest rise in roof height to improve interior space, the additional power was enough to yield a new top speed of 180mph (290km/h) in the new LP500S.

The Countach was so far ahead of its time that a car which was first exhibited in 1971 literally became a poster child for the conspicuous consumption of the 1980s. It continued to evolve, sprouting ever more outrageous aerodynamic addenda – necessary to keep the show on the road after Alfieri and Marmiroli increased the stroke in 1985 and fitted four-valve cylinder heads, enabling the 5175cc Quattrovalvole model to boast 470bhp.

BELOW: Despite updates, including better trim, the interior dated much more than the exterior.

BELOW: Horacio Pagani restyled the Countach for its 25th Anniversary model, substantially revising the cooling intakes and ducting.

Under Chrysler's ownership, the model bowed out with the 1988 Countach Anniversary, engineered by Horacio Pagani and featuring extensive use of carbonfibre. While marque purists consider this celebration of Lamborghini's 25th year the ugliest of the Countach family, some of the more flamboyant styling features served to distract from the larger bumpers required

by new US safety regulations. It was also the biggest-selling Countach: 650 examples left the factory, almost as many as the first three models combined and narrowly eclipsing the 610 achieved by the Quattrovalvole.

Of greater concern to Lamborghini aficionados was what the giant US corporation planned to do with its new acquisition.

The Show Must Go On

The Road to Ruin

"I didn't buy Lamborghini because I want a company that produces 300 cars a year."

For all but 10 of its first 35 years in business, the Lamborghini car company was passed around between owners like a bargain box of chocolate brownies. Each proprietor brought particular ambitions and some were more invested in love for the brand than others. But all lacked the right combination of vision, willpower and resource to resolve the operation's deep-seated issues.

First to fall was the partnership of Georges-Henri Rossetti and René Leimer. As a general principle, human beings are fearful of change. Add to this the disposition of overly powerful trade unions to throw their weight around (an issue not confined to Italian industry in the 1970s) and the result was a vicious circle of stuttering production, indifferent build quality, slow sales and weak

OPPOSITE: When the limited-edition Diablo SE30 was launched to mark the company's 30th anniversary in 1993, Lamborghini was already on its fourth set of owners.

BELOW: Designed as an 'affordable' model, the Urraco failed to lure buyers away from the Porsche 911 and barely registered in the important US market.

cash flow. In Rossetti's general absence, Leimer and sales director Ubaldo Sgarzi shouldered the burden of administration, usually only accepting orders for Countachs after full payment in cash. Cleverly, to reduce transport costs, Sgarzi would often invite motoring journalists to test-drive newly built cars… all the way to their destination country. The customer received their car with 'delivery mileage' and Lamborghini received free publicity in the form of some of the decade's most evocative travel writing.

To comply with tougher US safety and emissions laws, and similarly tighter type-approval regulations in Europe, the owners had to invest. Hence, Giampaolo Dallara's return as a consultant after Lamborghini stalwarts Paolo Stanzani and Bob Wallace left in 1975. He had two main problems to resolve: the wayward road manners of early Countach models (*see* Chapter 3) and the forthcoming obsolescence of the Espada and slow-selling Urraco.

Stanzani had engineered the Urraco cleverly to bring it in at an affordable price point, using many standard parts bought in

from BMW, Mercedes and Fiat. Its stylish Gandini-designed body looked the part and the driving experience attracted positive reviews – but the car never recovered from the two-year hiatus between 'reveal' and production, during which many buyers cancelled their orders. The transverse mid-mounted V8's performance was also underwhelming until it was expanded to 3 litres in late 1974, by which time Ferrari's 308 had arrived and set the bar even higher. A specially adapted version for the US market, with larger bumpers and a detuned engine to comply with new rules there, proved barely worth tooling up for – just 21 were sold.

ABOVE: The targa-roofed Silhouette was a clever repurposing of the Urraco, but it too failed to catch on.

Following the popularity of targa-roofed 308 and Porsche 911 models, Lamborghini's bosses directed Bertone and Dallara to rework the Urraco into a similar car that might finally conquer America. Shown as a prototype at the 1976 Turin show, the Silhouette even recycled the Urraco's doors and windscreen to

BELOW: Development issues and legal threats stymied the Cheetah project and worsened the company's financial position.

reduce tooling costs. Dallara and new chief engineer Franco Baraldini reworked the chassis for greater stiffness, adding a roll bar to compensate for the loss of the roof panel, and adopted new suspension geometry to maximize the potential of Pirelli's new P7 low-profile rubber. Another key area of concern was the interior, where the previously poor fit and finish had been a major turn-off for customers – especially in the USA.

Chasing opportunities elsewhere, Lamborghini entered two partnerships that offered extraordinary potential but ultimately plunged the company into financial turmoil. It reached a deal with BMW to manufacture the M1, a new Giugiaro-styled performance car, and committed to co-develop an off-road vehicle codenamed Cheetah with the US military contractor Mobility Technology International. The M1 might have been niche, but BMW had a deal to run a one-make race series for it on the Formula 1 support card, plus it needed to build 400 examples to homologate it for the World Sportscar

Championship; similarly, the continuing tensions in the Middle East had created demand for armoured rapid-attack vehicles.

These deals were enough to secure a $1.5 million grant from the Italian government, but both projects went south. Poor labour relations hit production of the M1 as well as the Silhouette and Countach, prompting BMW to shift production elsewhere. (One recipient of a contract was the UK racing organization Project 4, run by Ron Dennis; money from this project enabled him to employ visionary designer John Barnard to start on what would become the first composite-tub Formula 1 car, after Project 4's merger with McLaren in 1980.) The Cheetah, powered by a rear-mounted waterproofed 5.9-litre Chrysler V8 after Dallara abandoned a 7-litre version of the Lamborghini V12, was a hit at the 1977 Geneva show, but testing revealed it needed much more development. (In his autobiography, test driver Valentino Balboni recalled a truck coming the other way generating enough air pressure to pop all four doors out.) An intellectual property lawsuit from another putative military contractor over similarities with its own project hurried the Cheetah concept into extinction.

Scrambling for more cash, Leimer obtained a loan from US businessman and Countach owner Zoltan Reti, secured on the factory. Reti soon demanded his money back and had the company declared bankrupt. Fortunately for Lamborghini the receiver, Alessandro Artese, was a car aficionado who believed it *might* just be possible for the company to survive as a going concern and find a new buyer. Lamborghini also became the beneficiary of another Italian marque's woes: troubled Maserati had come under the control of Alejandro De Tomaso, who had cut half the workforce. Giulio Alfieri, an engineer who had a hand in the legendary 1950s Maserati 'Birdcage' as well as finessing the likes of the Merak and Bora, reputedly arrived for work one day to find the contents of his office in the car park. Artese wasted no time in appointing him managing director of Lamborghini. Alfieri prudently abandoned production of all Lamborghini models bar the Countach, which proceeded on a cash-upfront basis. This was not enough to save the company from ruin. It was a much, much humbler machine that came to the rescue.

The industrious Alfieri noticed that one of the many overseas-market derivatives of the Fiat 127 'supermini', the Brazilian Fiat 147, was sold with raised suspension and additional anti-rust measures to suit the country's often treacherously rutted roads outside urban spaces. He pitched Fiat on the idea of a 'ruggedized' 127 for the Italian market with faux off-road styling touches such as bull bars and chunky wheels. Fiat agreed and contracted Lamborghini to build 5,000 examples of what would be sold (in Italy only) as the 127 Rústica, handing the company a financial lifeline and enabling Alfieri to re-employ many workers left destitute by Lamborghini's insolvency.

Alfieri was also able to quietly work on a 'new' model, a cut-price revamp of the Silhouette. Though that model died after just 50 examples had found buyers, Alfieri remained confident that an affordable open-top Lamborghini should sell. Marc Deschamps, Marcello Gandini's successor at Bertone, had caught the eye with the Silhouette-based Athon concept car demonstrated on Bertone's stand at the 1980 Turin show. Alfieri commissioned the company to revise the Silhouette with the emphasis on integrating safety features (such as large bumpers) necessary for the US market. More extensive use of leather in the interior and an increase in engine capacity to 3485cc completed the transformation. Peak power remained at a claimed 255bhp, but the V8 achieved that output 500rpm earlier and enjoyed a fatter torque curve – the peak going from 130lb-ft to 232 – which made for a substantially different driving experience.

In badging this car the Jalpa, Lamborghini returned to the tradition of naming models after fighting bulls. Although a meagre 410 would be sold over 10 years in production, its mere existence at the time was significant. During the Jalpa's short development Lamborghini found new owners: African sugar barons Patrick and Jean-Claude Mimran, who arrived at the factory for the first time dressed in jeans and T-shirts.

In a complicated piece of financial engineering the assets of Automobili Lamborghini changed hands for $3 million in January 1981, transferring to a new legal entity, Nuova Automobili Ferruccio Lamborghini SpA, of which 24-year-old Patrick was the president. The transaction involved sacking the workforce and rehiring them the following day, a move which did much to bring the more febrile elements into line.

Just two months after the acquisition, Lamborghini emphasized its fresh start with a Geneva show line-up that included the new Jalpa and a second stab at the Cheetah concept, the LM001, produced in response to an expression of

BELOW: Working with minimal funds, Lamborghini revised the Silhouette and relaunched it as the Jalpa in 1981. Though sales ultimately proved disappointing, the Jalpa's mere existence was enough to impress the company's new owners.

ABOVE: Beloved of customers from royalty to drug lords, the LM002 was ugly and failed to interest its target market – but it caught a moment in the 1980s.

interest from Saudi Arabia. The rear-engined layout proved unsuitable for desert use – Balboni escaped a roll-over incident during testing near Jeddah – and the Mimrans pushed ahead with development of an all-new model. The resulting LMA002, shown a year later, now had the 4.8-litre V12 from the Countach LP500S sitting in the front of a spaceframe chassis which now had the room for ten occupants rather than four. Despite much-improved off-road performance, the car became a victim of timing as the key customers, Saudi Arabia and Kuwait, became distracted by the onset of the Iran–Iraq War.

Still the Mimrans persisted and the off-road concept would have its moment, though not with the clientele originally envisaged. As the inflationary, recession-speckled 1970s diminished in the rear-view mirror, the booming global economy triggered a new era of conspicuous consumption and displays of wealth. At the 1986 Brussels motor show Lamborghini revealed the LM002, still angular (enabling armour plating to be fitted) and rugged but more luxurious inside, and now powered by the latest 5.2-litre V12 from the Countach Quattrovalvole – albeit with a lower compression ratio to make it sympathetic to lower-octane fuel.

Rapidly nicknamed 'the Rambo Lambo' after the film character played by Sylvester Stallone, the LM002 attracted a constituency of people who liked to stand apart from commoners. Royalty, actors (including Stallone himself), rock stars, dictators and criminals flocked to sign on the dotted line. The Sultan of Brunei placed an order. Even Colombian drug lord Pablo Escobar kept one to patrol his private estate.

Even if market conditions had become favourable independently of Lamborghini's owners, the Mimrans had done well – and they cashed out to the tune of $33 million in May 1987, selling the company to Chrysler. Lido Anthony 'Lee' Iacocca, a self-styed titan of the automotive industry, was credited with turning the Chrysler corporation around after negotiating a government bailout in 1979. One of the pillars of this renaissance was a restructuring of the corporation's brands to use shared components and platforms, reducing costs at the expense of individuality. Fundamental to this was the front-engined K platform, introduced in 1981 and, by 1987, underpinning many Dodges, Plymouths and Chryslers. Iacocca's '87 shopping spree also included the struggling American Motor Corporation, whose brands were soon rolled into the mothership.

> *"I didn't buy Lamborghini because I want a company that produces 300 cars a year,"* Iacocca told his executive team. *"There's tremendous value in the brand. I want you guys to figure out what to do with it."*

The Mimrans had ceased 'unnecessary' spending in advance of the sale, leaving plans for successors to the Jalpa and Countach

M105 SDP

in limbo. Iacocca's agenda did not necessarily include rescuing them from it, either.

The initial signs were good. Chrysler designer Kevin Verduyn had produced a concept model called the Navajo the previous year and reworked it into a full-size vehicle for display at the Frankfurt motor show in late 1987. Based on Jalpa mechanicals, including the engine, and built by Carrozzeria Coggiola of Turin, it featured a pair of opposed scissor doors on each side granting access to a full four-seater cabin. Was this a pointer to a future Lamborghini model? No, but it was an indicator that Detroit would be calling the shots on design.

It was also becoming horrifyingly clear to the 'car guys' on the executive floor that Iacocca's real plans for the Lamborghini name were tantamount to blasphemy: he saw the bull logo as just another piece of tinsel which could be added to a badge-engineered high-profit stock platform. As part of a deliberate programme of 'malicious obedience' which included back-door involvement in Formula 1 (*see* Chapter 5), design chief Tom Gale took one of the most ostentatious K-platform models – the Chrysler Imperial – and made it even more ghastly by adding Lamborghini wheels, painting the whole ensemble bright red, fitting pale leather upholstery and adding Lamborghini logos to more or less any flat surface.

This monstrosity helped persuade the board that devaluing the brand would cost more in the long term, so the Countach and Jalpa replacements exited their stasis as part of a new strategy to grow Lamborghini's volume quickly. The deadline for the new Countach – the Diablo – was set unrealistically early: 1988.

Marcello Gandini returned as designer and his proposal was suitably dramatic, with an exaggerated rear deck bearing large air scoops, and sweeping flat-topped rear wheel arches. Chrysler's board did not like it and, as part of a wider operational schism between Sant'Agata and Detroit, Gale's team began reshaping

OPPOSITE TOP: Development of what became the Diablo was 'frozen' before the Chrysler takeover – and nearly left in the deep freeze.

OPPOSITE BOTTOM: The Diablo's rear deck and wheel arches were more 'conventional' than originally proposed after Chrysler's stylists adapted Marcello Gandini's original designs.

OVERLEAF: To stimulate flagging sales in the recession of the early 1990s, Megatech launched the Diablo SV, stripped out but with a more powerful engine than the standard car – and less expensive too.

SV

BELOW: To remain competitive the venerable Bizzarrini V12 had to grow to 5.7 litres.

OPPOSITE: Although dynamically the Diablo was an improvement on the Countach, the interior remained cramped and uncomfortable.

the car to smooth off the edges even as Balboni was starting to test a disguised prototype in Italy early in 1989. While the envelope of the Diablo remained unfixed, these tests did serve to demonstrate that it needed more power to beat newer competitors. Accordingly, the venerable V12 grew from 5.3 litres to 5.7.

While Gandini was irked by having the design taken out of his hands, enough to sell his original sketches to start-up supercar manufacturer Cizeta-Moroder (co-financed by music producer Giorgio Moroder), he deemed the final Diablo good enough to allow his signature to be appended to the flanks of production models. Not only was the Chryslerized Diablo less self-consciously edgy, it looked less bulky around the hips than the initial designs and features such as the coolant intakes were more neatly integrated. It was timeless enough to stay in production for over a decade before a minor facelift.

The Diablo was longer and taller than the Countach, and

ABOVE: The Diablo VT Roadster featured a removeable lightweight roof panel which could be fixed to the engine cover; an electric folding mechanism was shelved during development.

more lavishly upholstered. Heavier, too, since the underpinnings had to be strengthened to meet new crash regulations and handle the additional power. But it was substantially slipperier, having a drag coefficient of 0.31 compared with the late-model Countach's 0.42. Lamborghini claimed a top speed of 202mph (325km/h), while Balboni later admitted he had clocked that only after removing the mirrors and rear wing.

Deliveries began in September 1990. Once again Lamborghini suffered from poor market timing: the boom of the 1980s had turned to bust as Japan went into recession and tempers flared in the Middle East once again. When Iraq invaded neighbouring Kuwait, the price of oil doubled. Chrysler had taken on debt to fund Iacocca's acquisition spree and was now forced to unwind it, offloading Gulfstream Aerospace and instructing the investment bank J. P. Morgan to value

Lamborghini for sale. The mooted new Jalpa, codenamed P140, went into hiatus and Lamborghini struggled to fund the four-wheel-drive Diablo VT model. An open-top Diablo Roadster prototype designed by Gandini appeared at the 1992 Geneva show, but would not go into production while Chrysler's logo remained on the company notepaper.

In January 1994 Chrysler sold to a consortium of three Bermuda-based, Indonesian-owned companies (all ultimately owned by Hutomo 'Tommy' Mandala Putra, the son of Indonesian President Suharto) and the multimillionaire Setiawan Djody for a reported $40 million. Djody intended to use this as a platform to create a new car for the Indonesian market under the Megatech brand, though this would ultimately come to naught when Suharto was ousted in 1997 during the wider Asian economic crisis.

The Megatech era began optimistically enough for Giugiaro's ItalDesign company to make a styling pitch for the putative Jalpa replacement, exhibiting the Calà concept vehicle on its stand at the 1995 Geneva show. Nothing came of this – for now – and, indeed, not much eventuated from the Megatech era bar a number of Diablo special editions and the much-delayed Roadster model. Former Lotus and General Motors Executive Mike Kimberley came and went, frustrated as promises of investment in new models failed to materialize and Megatech chose retrenchment and cost-cutting instead.

Kimberley's replacement, former Fiat executive Vittorio Di Capua, dispatched chief engineer Maurizio Reggiani to the Volkswagen Audi Group with a view to using its 4.2-litre V8 engine and Quattro four-wheel drivetrain in a rebooted P140 project. Rather more would come of these tentative negotiations than that…

OPPOSITE: Unlike the Countach, the Diablo had one-piece retracting door windows. On the SE30 model, the electric mechanism was removed to save weight and the windows replaced by plexiglass with a sliding inset panel.

BELOW: ItalDesign's Calà was a fully functional prototype, but Lamborghini's owners lacked the funds or ambition to build it.

The Audi Renaissance

Bigger, Better, Faster, More

"The Murciélago undisputedly still remains relevant, or as relevant as a 212mph 1.7-tonne two-seat lorry can be."

Lamborghini's approach during the Megatech era to the Volkswagen Group to use Audi's V8 engine and Quattro drivetrain in the long-gestating P140 project resulted in the opportunity for the financially troubled owners to divest. VW overlord Ferdinand Piëch, grandson of Ferdinand Porsche and chief engineer of the Le Mans-winning Porsche 917 racer, was in accumulation mode thanks to the group's expanding mainstream market share. He had already snapped up Bugatti and was negotiating to acquire Bentley, chiefly to keep it out of rival BMW's hands. News that Lamborghini's owners were wavering provided an irresistible opportunity to bring another potentially lucrative premium brand into the fold.

In June 1998, after protracted negotiations, Audi bought Lamborghini for a reported $110 million – rather less than the $790

OPPOSITE: To launch the Murciélago within three years of Audi buying Lamborghini meant the new car had to be based on the Diablo's chassis architecture.

million VW would ultimately pay to steer Bentley away from Munich. Within months a facelifted version of the Diablo was released, but the legwork on this – including the replacement of the pop-up lights with cheaper, simpler fixed units bought in from Nissan – had been done before the takeover. The wider automotive world would have to wait a little longer to work out what Piëch's people planned.

During the extensive due-diligence process, Audi calculated that Lamborghini would have to sell 1,500 units per year to balance the books – a figure hitherto unseen during the procession of different owners. Costs could be cut, yes, through that dread word 'synergies' – using as many existing parts as possible, preferably hidden, just as Paolo Stanzani had done with the Urraco but on a larger and more organized scale from within the wider VW empire. Given the direction of travel Lamborghini nearly took under Chrysler, marque aficionados were right to be concerned about what agenda the new owners might have. But it was never part of the plan to simply slap Lamborghini badges on humdrum saloons and sell them at a premium.

Obviously a new tentpole model would be required to replace the Diablo. But a more affordable one would also be required – along the lines of the Urraco, Jalpa, and so on, though this one would have to achieve more traction in the market.

Lamborghini had been tentatively working on a new Diablo, to be called the Canto. Carrozzeria Zagato, one of the last independent Italian coachbuilding houses, had provided a design for this as well as presenting the Raptor concept car. Marcello Gandini had also produced a proposal called the Acosta. Piëch ordered these scrapped in favour of an all-new concept to be generated by Belgian-born designer Luc Donckerwolke, who had styled the first new models to be built by Skoda, another of VW's acquisitions. Donckerwolke would become the first Lamborghini design chief of the Audi era.

Audi set an ambitious launch date of 2001 for the Diablo replacement, now to be called the Murciélago, after a fighting bull said to have been brought into the Miura line as a sire after surviving 90 sword strokes. While that figure was debatable, the resonance with Lamborghini's recent history was clear. In the meantime, Lamborghini fettled the Diablo with a final flurry of updates which would pave the way for its successor: not only was the engine brought out to 6 litres, the pedal box was redesigned to free up more space in the footwell and improve the driving experience.

Though timescales dictated extensive use of the existing Diablo chassis architecture, Donckerwolke's Murciélago

BELOW: The Murciélago cleverly and respectfully integrated design themes from the Countach and Diablo into a contemporary style.

ABOVE: Ergonomics and interior quality vastly improved under Audi's ownership.

design was a masterstroke, setting a clear direction for future Lamborghinis while incorporating enough familiar themes to demonstrate Audi's respect for the brand. It also avoided many of the potential pitfalls encountered by other designers in terms of accommodating the engineering requirements such as cooling. It was neat and modern but also unmistakably a Lamborghini – and the underpinnings, too, were unimpeachably the work of Sant'Agata, including a new six-speed gearbox transmitting power from the latest 6.2-litre version of the Bizzarrini/ Dallara V12 through to Lamborghini's own four-wheel-drive transmission. Road-testers criticized the brakes on early models, and the cramped footwell remained a bugbear, but in 2002 alone 424 Murciélagos left the factory – well over a hundred more sales than the Diablo had accomplished annually.

Fast-tracking the new entry-level model to production entailed some compromises. In early 2000, Audi invited styling proposals from Donckerwolke's new in-house studio as well as Italdesign, Bertone and IDEA. To enable Lamborghini

Centro Stile to focus on the Murciélago, management selected Italdesign's pitch, essentially an updated version of the 1995 Calà show car. Its winning touch was that this concept had been a runner, with a spaceframe chassis and a Lamborghini-built V10 produced during the Chrysler era. Reduced in size and finessed by Donckerwolke to harmonize its look with the Murciélago, this would become the Gallardo – a mic drop to established competition including Ferrari's 360 and Porsche's venerable 911.

Audi declared the original V10 unsuitable, which left Lamborghini to design a new one based on the architecture of Audi's V8, mated to a new multivalve cylinder head created in partnership with Cosworth. Though early Gallardos attracted criticism for their standards of fit and finish, truculent 'e-gear' robotized manual gearbox and excessive clutch wear, there were compelling reasons for this: by the winter of 2002–03, just a few

BELOW: The Gallardo succeeded where the Urraco, Silhouette and Jalpa had failed, achieving record sales figures for the company.

months before deliveries were due to begin, the production line was still being installed, so many elements had to be outsourced. The aluminium spaceframes were fabricated in Germany by Krupp-Drauz and then painted at an Audi facility, the former NSU plant at Neckarsulm.

Despite its teething issues, the Gallardo was considered a threatening enough competitor for Ferrari to bring forward the launch of its 360 Modena replacement, the F430, by a whole 18 months. The F430 was 70kg (154lb) lighter than the Gallardo, chiefly by doing without all-wheel drive, and boasted a power output just 10bhp shy of the Lamborghini's 493bhp. The 360 Modena had made do with 394bhp.

As road-testers began to compare the Gallardo unfavourably with the more agile and responsive F430, Lamborghini hit back with revisions for the 2006 model year, plus a Superleggera model 100kg (220lb) lighter, before launching a second-generation model in 2008. Mildly facelifted, lightened and now featuring an all-new 5.2-litre V10, the latest Gallardo also incorporated Lamborghini's new designation format in its name – LP560-4, shorthand for the location and alignment of the engine, metric horsepower output and number of driven wheels. Spyder models broadened the car's appeal and, when the final Gallardo was built in November 2013, the company marked the occasion with a special ceremony for management and staff. Over a decade in production, 14,022 Gallardos had been built and sold, making this Lamborghini's most successful model until the Urus overtook it.

The Murciélago also kept Ferrari honest throughout its life. A Roadster model joined the line-up in 2004 and Lamborghini kept the refreshes coming – a necessary strategy, as the performance war with Maranello kicked off by the Gallardo meant theoretically lesser machinery began to hustle in its wheeltracks. A 2006 refresh included a 6.5-litre evolution of the V12, now peaking at 631bhp, but the limitations of the old-fashioned chassis construction were beginning to show.

"*The Murciélago undisputedly still remains relevant,*" said *Car* magazine's road test of the new LP640, "*or as relevant as a 212mph 1.7-tonne two-seat lorry can be.*"

Audi's response was two-pronged. For the long term it greenlit development of a successor model to be based around a composite structure rather than a steel spaceframe. It also signed off on the limited-edition Reventón, essentially a reskinned Murciélago with a mildly tweaked engine and composite body panels. The jet fighter-style design touches were as eye-grabbing as the colour, a grey which was both matt-finish and subtly metallic.

Anyone who thought this super-rarefied model, of which only 20 would be built, was a ridiculous fashion accessory for the super-rich was only half right. Megaprofits lay not in devaluing a brand by splashing its badge across humbler models, but by adopting a couture-style approach. The parallel business model that Lamborghini was about to adopt was hinted at in the VW Group's 2007 annual report:

> *"The idea behind this strictly limited edition of 20 vehicles was to create a model that would crown the success of the brand, that will serve as a four-wheeled ambassador for the uniqueness of Lamborghini – and that will also demonstrate the short development times of which the sports car manufacturer is now capable."*

The world might have been in recession again in 2009 when Lamborghini unveiled the €1.1million Reventón Roadster at the Frankfurt show, but 12 of the 15 examples had already been sold to 'friends and collectors'. The company would return to this lucrative watering hole again and again over the coming decade and a half, spinning out bespoke one-offs and limited editions for high net worth individuals.

BELOW: The Reventón signalled Lamborghini's move to develop high-profit, limited-edition supercars based on existing models.

ABOVE: Everything about the Aventador was new, from its composite chassis to an engine which shared only its swept volume with the classic Bizzarrini V12.

The post-2008 global financial crisis did impinge on the buying habits of those slightly further down the income scale as Murciélago sales diminished towards the end of its life, although many buyers might simply have been waiting on its successor. Though just half of the planned 350 units were built and sold of the run-off LP670-4 SV model, during its nine-year lifetime 4,099 Murciélagos were made – over 1,000 more than the Diablo had achieved in 11 years.

To keep pace with competition, which now included F1 constructor McLaren, Lamborghini had to embrace a new construction format in the Aventador, launched in 2011 and named after a fighting bull which met its maker in a celebrated bout in 1993. Chasing the future also meant bidding farewell to a cherished element of the company's history, the Bizzarrini/Dallara V12. The new-generation V12 remained at 6.5 litres but was revvier and had more torque, thanks to wider bore dimensions and a shorter stroke. Peak power of 691bhp (a gain from its predecessor's 632) came higher up the rev range than before, amplifying the inherent aggression in the engine's character. A new seven-speed automated manual gearbox boasted shift times of just 50 milliseconds while weighing less than Volkswagen's 'seamless shift' twin-clutch DSG.

Filippo Perini, Donckerwolke's successor at Centro Stile, was responsible for styling that once again deliberately invoked the look and function of fighter jets. Beneath the extrovert bodywork lay a composite monocoque chassis with aluminium carriers for the suspension and engine, the better to ensure cost-effective repairability after minor accidents. Relocating the radiators to the sides of the car enabled Perini to integrate the aircraft-style air scoops into the flanks rather than having boxy projections at shoulder level. All in all the Aventador weighed

BELOW: Just as the exterior of contemporary Lamborghinis have taken inspiration from fighter jets, so too has the interior design.

ABOVE: To mark the company's 50th anniversary Lamborghini crossed an Aventador with a Le Mans-style race car. Just three were built, for sale at $4million.

OPPOSITE: Another 50th anniversary special was the jet-fighter-inspired Egoista, a one-off built (supposedly from anti-radar materials) to accommodate just one person.

90kg (198lb) less than the Murciélago. The Roadster model launched in 2013 incurred a 50kg (110lb) weight gain as a result of the additional bracing required, though this was less of an inconvenience than the dilemma of where to stow the carbonfibre roof panels – once inside the car, they took up all the luggage space.

"*What do we do with our luggage*," an American journalist asked CEO Stephan Winkelmann at the Aventador Roadster's launch. "*Send it by FedEx?*"

Winkelmann was able to brush off the question, safe in the knowledge that the 2000th Aventador had already left the production line. Lamborghini had only ever sold 2,042 Countachs. A mid-life refresh by new chief designer Mitja Borkert, along with continuous engineering revisions and a power boost to 730bhp, meant the Aventador retained its place among the state-of-the-art until it bowed out in 2022, by which time 3,196 Roadsters and 11,819 coupés had been delivered.

STEP
HERE
FOR EMERGENCY RESCUE
BREAK GLASS
JET FUEL ONLY

ABOVE: Replacing the Gallardo, the Huracán developed the stealth aircraft styling theme while featuring more synergies with high-end Audi products.

The Aventador also provided a handy donor vehicle for Lamborghini's side hustle of building super-limited editions such as the Centenario and Veneno, leading onto the bespoke tailoring service which produced the SC20 – a one-off which Borkert styled to a customer's order. Likewise the Gallardo donated running gear to rarities such as the Egoista show car (built to celebrate the company's 50th anniversary) and the carbonfibre showcase that was the $6.5million Sesto Elemento (believed to have sold no more than 10 of the planned 20).

In following up the Gallardo with the Huracán, Lamborghini collaborated with Audi engineers to develop the MSS (Modular

Sportscar System) platform which would underpin the next-generation R8, among others. Its spaceframe structure is part-steel, part composite, with panels made using Lamborghini's patented resin-transfer process. Despite Sant'Agata's involvement, Audi's R&D chief Dr Ulrich Hackenberg was a highly unwelcome presence at the Huracán launch, where he repeatedly sought to remind the audience how much Audi DNA was present in the car. Nevertheless the Huracán took just five years to reach the sales figures the Gallardo achieved in ten.

OVERLEAF: It took the flamboyant Huracán just five years to equal its predecessor's sales figures.

Enthusiasts cavil, but SUVs are now a vital element of any car manufacturer's model portfolio. In 2012 Lamborghini displayed

KELUAR

IKEA
IKEA
Lamborghini

BELOW: The limited-edition off-road Huracán Sterrato attracted rave reviews and sold out so quickly that the production run was increased from 900 to 1499.

OPPOSITE: While many car enthusiasts profess to loathe SUVs, they are an essential part of any manufacturer's range. The Urus is Lamborghini's best-selling model ever.

the prototype Urus at the Beijing show. Supposedly powered by the Gallardo V10, the concept car was in fact a non-runner – and the final production vehicle was the result of a judicious raid on the VW parts bin by Maurizio Reggiani and his team. Tweaked only slightly by Borkert from Perini's original look, the Urus launched in December 2017 sat on the same VW MLB-evo platform as the Porsche Cayenne, VW Touraeg, Audi Q8 and Bentley Bentayga. In the engine bay sat a 4-litre twin-turbo Audi V8 reworked to produce 640bhp. Polarizing it may be, but the Urus sold over 15,000 units in its first four years.

In 2022, despite war in Ukraine and a chilly global economic climate, Lamborghini delivered 9,233 cars – six times the figure of a target once considered out of reach. But it now faced the same difficult choices as rival high-performance car builders: how to stay relevant as the world's supply of fossil fuels dwindled.

Electric Dreams

Facing the Future

"A Lamborghini super-sports car is driven maybe 3,000 miles a year, not every day, so electrification has to offer an added intensity to justify its inclusion."

The inevitability that declining fossil fuel resources will make oil more expensive – and conspicuous consumption of it more problematic – is a challenge for the entire automotive industry and a bitterly divisive issue for its customers. An existential threat, too, for brands such as Lamborghini which are predicated upon an intoxicating combination of performance and spectacle. In this market space, noise is a powerful element of the desirability factor – or at least it has been until recently. And the customer base for big-beast V10 and V12 sports cars is not one for whom the cost of a tank of fuel is an issue (indeed, many hail from those parts of the world where black gold is still pumped from beneath the ground in large quantities).

OPPOSITE: Lamborghini showed the hybrid-boosted 900bhp Asterion in 2014 but abandoned production in favour of the Urus.

ABOVE: All-electric and powered by supercapacitors rather than lithium ion batteries, the Terzo Millennio was theoretically capable of 186mph (299km/h).

All the more reason for Lamborghini to take small steps at first. The world got a first look at what a hybrid-powered Lamborghini might look like at the 2014 Paris motor show. It left largely unimpressed. Based on an Aventador monocoque, the Asterion had a two-door composite bodyshell and was powered by a Huracán-derived V10 augmented by three brushless electric motors. Though theoretical peak power was 898bhp, CO_2 emissions were nearly a quarter of the Aventador and Lamborghini described the Asterion as "*conceived more for comfortable luxury daily cruising than for ultimate track performance*."

This sounds more like the preserve of the Urraco and sundry other vintage Lamborghinis which failed to find an audience, which may explain what happened next. CEO Stephan Winkelmann admitted that the lukewarm customer reaction prompted him to drop plans to put the Asterion into production and shift the budget towards the Urus instead.

"They told us that they were open to innovation, including hybrid technology, but only if it came with the benefit of added performance," he said.

"A Lamborghini super-sports car is driven maybe 3,000 miles a year, not every day, so electrification has to offer an added intensity to justify its inclusion."

This was not quite a slamming of the door on electrified Lamborghinis, but it was obvious that Winkelmann and the board were struggling to see a future which did not involve V12s. Market shifts, along with governments worldwide taking an increasingly hostile position on the internal combustion engine, would force the company's hand. In particular, Elon Musk's electric-car challenger brand Tesla began to rake in sales among wealthier customers who liked to signal they were forward-thinking.

Lamborghini joined the rush of manufacturers showing EV hypercar concepts in 2017. The Terzo Millennio – 'third millennium' – fulfilled the company's long tradition of majoring on the wow factor. Its ostentatious shell, Mitja Borkert's first clean-sheet design since slipping his feet under the desk at Centro Stile, was just part of the drama. Underneath it used supercapacitors rather than traditional lithium ion batteries to power four electric motors which could, theoretically, propel the Terzo Millennio to 186mph (299km/h). Developed in conjunction with the Massachusetts Institute of Technology and publicly unveiled there, the car was the first product of an ongoing partnership researching future technologies such as self-healing body panels and the integration of the electrical power transfer into the structure of the car.

Supercapacitor technology also underpinned Lamborghini's next electrification project, the company's most powerful road car ever until that point. Based on Aventador SVJ donor elements, the Sián FKP37 (named after a Bolognese dialect word for a lightning bolt, together with Ferdinand Piéch's initials and

ABOVE: Dramatic as the Sián was, it was essentially an Aventador SVJ with a hybrid kick.

date of birth) could accelerate from 0 to 62mph in 2.8 seconds. And it was popular – every one of the 63 examples of this $3.3million speed machine was sold before the public unveiling at Frankfurt in 2019.

Many industry figures derided the Sián FKP37 as possibly Lamborghini's most cynical high-margin limited edition yet, so much did it have in common with the donor car. But Lamborghini was about to be yet more provocative, announcing a hybridized reboot of the Countach (just three years after Winkelmann had announced "*retro design is not what we are here for*"). Also based on the Aventador platform and running a Sián-based 800bhp four-wheel-drive powertrain, it was announced as a 112-car limited edition – a figure based on the original's

conceptual designation 'Project 112' – during Monterey Car Week in August 2021. Priced at $2.5million, substantially more for those who failed to exercise self-control while perusing the options list, the Countach LPI 800-4 also sold out before its launch – despite *Road & Track* magazine branding it "*a cynical cash grab aimed at ultra-wealthy collectors*".

Rather more of a hit with media and the customer base, the Revuelto – launched in 2023 as the Aventador replacement – signalled an end to Lamborghini's apparent policy of stamping its hooves in the face of electrification. The new-generation L545 V12 remains on the large side (6.5 litres) but weighs 17kg (37lb) more than that which propelled the Aventador. Three electric motors, two of which propel the front wheels

BELOW: The Revuelto features detailed lightweighting and a hybrid powertrain and is essentially Lamborghini's first 'proper' mainstream electrified vehicle.

(helping to save weight by eliminating 4WD running gear) are responsible for 187 of the total claimed 814bhp and help push the car from rest to 62mph in 2.5 seconds. While each motor is capable of providing 148bhp, in practice this is constrained by the use of small battery packs to save some weight.

Lamborghini's first all-electric vehicle is also on the horizon. Due in 2028, the Lanzador will be a 2+2 coupé presented in

modish SUV proportions, powered by two electric motors outputting the equivalent of 1,340bhp. A concept version presented in 2023 featured an off-the-shelf electric powertrain for dynamic photography purposes only; at the time of writing Lamborghini has not ruled out incorporating some form of augmented engine noise. It will not, however, offer a synthesis of the original V12. That one will have to live on in the memory only.

OVERLEAF: With the Revuelto, Lamborghini has faced up to electrification without compromising on drama.

Lamborghini at the Races

NACIONAL
NACIONAL

The Bull Enters the Ring

"The fastest way to make a small fortune in motor racing is to start off with a large one."

Before the mobile phone there was the car phone, a piece of kit so costly to install and run in its heyday that it unequivocally signalled the owner as a person of means – a person of *business*. So, naturally, McLaren Formula 1 team boss Ron Dennis, a man whose entrepreneurial drive, punctilious attention to detail and sheer energy for breaking boundaries had done so much to establish F1 as the cutting edge of motorsport technology, had one of these executive tools close at hand in his chauffeur-driven limo.

On 23 September 1993 it buzzed with a call of singular importance. "*Ron, hi, it's Ayrton*," said the voice at the other end of the line. The unmistakable Brazilian-accented timbre rendered the introduction superfluous. Of course it was Ayrton Senna, three-time world champion, arguably the greatest racing driver alive. And Ayrton had something to say: he was very, very excited by the Lamborghini-engined McLaren F1 car he had just tested.

OPPOSITE: Ayrton Senna tested a McLaren F1 car adapted to house Lamborghini's V12 – but the partnership never came to fruition.

McLaren and Lamborghini are one of Formula 1's great 'woulda couldas shoulda' and yet this test – indeed Lambo's entire foray into F1 – are now footnotes to history. It would never have happened in Ferruccio Lamborghini's day; one of the many traits which separated him from Enzo Ferrari was that while he was a keen driver (if not, according to those close to him, as skilled as he believed himself to be), he had little passion for or appetite to become involved in motorsport. This firm red line in his thinking was one of the factors which influenced the departure of Giampaolo Dallara and curtailed Lamborghini's relationship with Giotto Bizzarrini. A few miles away in Maranello, Enzo's company had always been racing first, road cars second – selling cars was just a means of funding the racing.

Ferruccio's coolness towards motorsport did not stop third parties – including some of his own staff – attempting to fettle his cars for racing purposes. After stepping up to the technical director role, Paolo Stanzani quietly allowed Bob Wallace to modify a standard Miura P400 by drilling out sections of the monocoque, replacing other steel elements of the chassis and bodywork for lightweight materials, redesigning the fuel system, adding race-spec suspension components and fettling the engine to deliver more power. Skirts and spoilers aimed to cure the Miura's chronic problem of aerodynamic lift generated by the bonnet profile. The resulting car – christened the Jota – remained the most powerful Miura built, its 440bhp output eclipsing even the later SV model.

However, it remained a one-off, apart from later conversions commissioned by customers; the original was crashed by an overenthusiastic driver, caught fire, and was damaged beyond repair. Though the Jota would likely have been competitive in sportscar racing, then a more lucrative arena than F1 in terms of prize money, the rules were in seemingly constant flux. Appendix J of the FIA regulations (popularly believed to have inspired the model's name) required manufacturers to build a minimum number – in the case of the grand touring class, 500, which was not a given in 1970. By the time production ceased in 1973, only 764 Miuras are believed to have been built.

Motorsport remained off-menu as Lamborghini's initial cycle of post-Ferruccio owners struggled to keep the marque afloat. In the mid-1980s David Jolliffe, a keen amateur racer and managing director of Lamborghini's UK importer, wanted to prepare a Countach LP5000S for competition in the Group B sportscar racing category but was thwarted by the minimum-build regulations. Merely inconvenienced by this obstacle, he set his sights on the more rarefied Group C and the world championship. Gordon Spice's eponymous engineering company created a bespoke chassis for what would become the Countach QVX – which looked nothing like the road car, though it was powered by a factory-modified version of its V12. North Yorkshire-based team CC Racing Developments, who had run Spice and Belgian privateer Teddy Pilette to victory in the 1978

BELOW: While the original Miura Jota was destroyed, the factory converted a handful of SV models to Jota spec – including this one for German Lamborghini importer Hubert Hahne.

ABOVE: Japanese racer Aguri Suzuki scored a career-best third place in his home grand prix in 1990. It would also be the best finish for a Lamborghini-powered car.

Spa 24 Hours, were tasked with race preparation, and sometime F1 drivers Mauro Baldi and Tiff Needell (who brought Unipart sponsorship) were engaged to drive. But money was always tight and the project fizzled out in early 1987 after contesting just one significant international event.

While this privateer sportscar programme evaporated, US car giant Chrysler was completing due diligence on its $25-million acquisition of Lamborghini, having already swallowed the American Motors Corporation. Executives, including design chief Tom Gale and head of global product development Bob Lutz, then set themselves the task of heading off Chrysler boss Lee Iacocca's plans to use the Lamborghini brand as a means of sprinkling gold dust on humdrum family cars.

Further impetus for the executive floor's programme of

'malicious obedience' to Iacocca came from François Castaing, the French engineer who had arrived at Chrysler via the AMC deal. Earlier in his career Castaing had been the architect of Renault's V6 turbo-powered Formula 1 entry and now he championed the cause of deploying Lamborghini's engineering potential as well as the value of the badge.

There would never be enough money in Castaing's engineering budget to support a Ferrari-style vertically integrated Formula 1 team, but he was able to divert funds towards an engine programme, with Lutz greasing the mechanism by selling Iacocca on it as a brand-bolstering exercise that would have particular value in Chrysler's planned return to Europe. The timing was right, since motorsport's governing body had signalled a direction of travel away from the turbo engines which

ABOVE: In 1991 Lamborghini unwittingly ended up as a Formula 1 entrant when a key sponsor ran off with the money

held sway in the 1980s, progressively limiting their potential via boost and fuel limits ahead of an outright ban in 1989.

The personnel were available too, since long-time Ferrari technical director Mauro Forghieri had quit after being sidelined in favour of the British engineer Harvey Postlethwaite. Working in a new company named Lamborghini Engineering, run by ex-Ferrari team manager Daniele Audetto, Forghieri set about creating an 80-degree, naturally aspirated 3.5-litre V12 with which to take on the nemesis from Maranello.

Limited financial resources hampered the F1 project at every step. The first iteration of the LE3512 engine was overweight and not reliable enough in comparison with competitors. Its deliberately low-key introduction in 1989 – an alliance with the midfield team run by ex-F1 driver Gerard Larrousse – netted little in the way of actual results. The Lola-designed chassis was only adequate, a description which also aptly suited the drivers: Philippe Alliot in one car and a rotating cast in the other.

1989 ended with just one points finish in the bag. Lamborghini's official history naturally blames Larrousse: "*The fault for these poor results lay above all with the French team, which did not have the money and organization required to compete at the highest levels.*" This rather overlooks the engine's tendency to blow up, as in the British Grand Prix, when Eric Bernard was running fifth before an almighty belch of smoke signalled that he would be returning to the pits on foot.

Despite the addition of the once-mighty Lotus team to the list of Lamborghini's F1 clients in 1990, the engine's best result came via Larrousse. Aguri Suzuki benefited from disarray at the head of the field to finish on the podium in front of his home crowd at Suzuka.

Forghieri had also been designing a Formula 1 car to accommodate the engine – not with money from Chrysler itself but on a promise from the Mexican GLAS (Gonzalez Luna Associates) consortium fronted by self-styled entrepreneur Fernando Gonzalez Luna. This entity raised a reputed $20 million from sponsors before Gonzalez Luna disappeared into the ether – along with the money – in the summer of 1990.

Thus Lamborghini faced a problem. Canning the project after a substantial sum had been spent would invite difficult questions from the US parent company. Proceeding was virtually out of the question, too, since Iacocca would never sanction the required investment. Keeping it in the wider family was an appropriately Italian solution: the financier and industrialist Carlo Petrucco was persuaded to open his wallet. And so, in 1991, the hitherto unheard-of Modena Team Lamborghini arrived on the Formula 1 entry list with a pair of metallic blue cars badged as Lamborghini 291s.

This was not an automatic ticket onto the grid, since the barriers to entry were not so high as they are in the twenty-first century. In 1991, the heady days before yet another global

OVERLEAF: Lamborghini's factory-supported team fizzled out through lack of investment. By the closing races of 1991 they were struggling to qualify for races – here Nicola Larini was five seconds slower than the pole position time for the Portuguese GP.

Bâtiments
& Ponts

Central Park
Lamborghini
Victors
HRF
GOODYEAR
34
EAGLE

BELOW: Although the Lamborghini V12 was longer and heavier than Ford's V8, Senna lapped faster with it and was impressed.

recession, F1 was oversubscribed and the newcomers and also-rans faced a brutal knock-out prequalifying session at an unsociably early hour on the Friday of each grand prix weekend. Like most low-budget F1 cars of the era, the 291 was some way short of the cutting edge and it survived prequalifying only occasionally. Nicola Larini got through and finished seventh at Phoenix, just one position short of the points; more frustrating still was when teammate Eric van de Poele was running fifth in the wet at Imola when his fuel pump broke in the closing laps.

"*What can I do?*" he asked his race engineer over the radio.

"*All you can do, Eric, is cry,*" came the response.

With no further financial support from Lamborghini in prospect, and in the absence of sufficient results to tempt sponsors, Modena Team faded from the scene and ceased operations at the end of the season. While the company's official history, naturally, blames Chrysler for this failure, what it does not report is that the parent company *did* take a greater interest

ABOVE: McLaren put a lot of effort into creating a 'mule car' to test the V12, but team boss Ron Dennis ultimately did a deal for Peugeot V10s.

in Lamborghini Engineering after this point, as Iacocca retired and handed over the reins to Bob Eaton. Forghieri was replaced by long-time company man (and Sports Car Club of America regional organizer) Michael Royce and, over the winter of 1992 into 1993, the V12 was significantly revised with input from US-based engineers and rebadged as the Chrysler-Lamborghini CL01.

It was this engine which so delighted Senna on that sunny autumn day in southern Portugal. To reach that point had taken three months of intensive work by McLaren and Lamborghini engineers to adapt an MP4/8 chassis to accommodate both the longer engine and the team's preference for in-house TAG Electronics control systems. But McLaren, left relying on second-string customer Ford V8s after Honda's withdrawal at the end of 1992, were desperate. The MP4/8 was one of the most competitive cars on the grid, good for grand prix wins in Senna's hands, even though down on power compared with rivals. Even in compromised form, hacked about with a longer, heavier engine shoehorned in, it lapped faster than when pushed

BELOW: With the Diablo SV-R, Lamborghini created a lucrative one-make race series for high net worth customers.

by Ford's V8 – though accounts vary as to by how much.

Senna filed a wish list of suggestions for improvements and it is claimed that Ron Dennis had gone as far as shaking hands with Lutz and Audetto at the Frankfurt motor show earlier in September… only to go cold on the putative alliance and sign up with Peugeot for 1994 instead. Some say the allure of receiving 'free' engines from a recent Le Mans 24 Hours winner trumped the option of having to pay for the Italian-built V12s; others say Dennis felt Chrysler and Lamborghini were not committed enough, a sense magnified by the fact that his test engines were not fresh but drawn from a pool already used by other F1 customers. A spectacular blow-up during a Silverstone

test, in which at least one connecting rod punched through the block, was the decider.

Perhaps Dennis's instincts were right: Lamborghini was already being hawked around for potential sale. The F1 programme would have been unlikely to survive the transition to new owners.

When MegaTech took over and installed ex-Lotus and GM man Mike Kimberley as president and managing director, one of Kimberley's initiatives was to spice up Lamborghini's sporting appeal at relatively low cost by reviving the SuperVeloce (SV) badge last seen on the hottest Miuras and applying it to the Diablo. More powerful and shorn of its all-wheel drive system,

ABOVE: Lamborghinis have also featured in the annual all-star Race of Champions event.

OPPOSITE: The Super Trofeo one-make series now has regional championships all over the world, pairing professional drivers with wealthy amateurs.

this was an altogether rawer driving experience – and it begat a stripped-out version, the SV-R, with which Lamborghini launched its one-make racing series, the Supertrophy. Ferrari had already used this tactic to 'sex up' the image of their initially underwhelming 348 model and make a profit at the same time: offering wealthy clients a turn-key racing experience in identical machinery. For £160,000 per year the company would supply, store, maintain and transport the cars to various circuits (initially in Europe), and all the owner-drivers had to do was present themselves in the right place at the appropriate weekends. From small beginnings the concept has evolved into the globe-straddling Super Trofeo Lamborghini runs (now with Huracáns) which continue to this day.

But it was not until the turn of the century, after Audi took over stewardship of the brand, that Lamborghini made a concerted assault on inter-marque competition – and once again at arm's length, this time with Reiter Engineering, the German tuner which prepared cars for the Supertrophy. Again it was a

motorsport
GAMES

ABOVE: Lamborghini is now taking on Ferrari in the top category of sportscar racing with the SC63 'hypercar'.

case of building from a relatively small scale with a GT1-class version of the Diablo, then the Murciélago, which matured into a race winner.

The catalyst for Lamborghini getting properly involved in racing was Reiter's success with the Gallardo, after the creation of the less rarefied GT3 class in 2006. Closer to the road cars than GT1s, these were more accessible for non-professional racers and more affordable – and sold in their tens and hundreds. In 2013 Lamborghini established an in-house racing division, Squadra Corse, to develop and build future GT3-class cars rather than selling parts to third parties. Over the past decade the Huracán, in various evolution models, has become one of the dominant forces in international racing, with customer teams the world over enjoying close support from the factory.

Now, after much political push-and-pull behind the scenes and a couple of false starts, the Lamborghini name will grace the top level of international sportscar racing in the World Endurance Championship's new hypercar class. The SC63, launched at the 2023 Goodwood Festival of Speed, features a hybrid powertrain in which a 3.8-litre V8 internal combustion engine is augmented by a 50kW electric motor driving the rear wheels. A complex balancing mechanism devised by the organizers aims to equalize the playing field between different cars while encouraging individual engineering touches.

Most significantly, as Lamborghini enters its seventh decade, this is the first time one of the company's cars will meet its Ferrari equivalent at the pinnacle of sportscar racing.

On the Big Screen

LAMBORGHINI

THE MAN BEHIND THE LEGEND

Stunt Casting

"Will you be wanting the Batpod, Sir?"
"It's the middle of the day Alfred – not very subtle."
"The Lamborghini, then. Much more subtle."

Cars carrying the bull insignia have become a distinct element in popular culture's visual grammar, signifying a brazen unsubtlety that (usually) falls just short of outright obnoxiousness. To cast a Lamborghini is to consciously send a very different set of messages to the audience than casting a Ferrari.

Those wishing to explore the brand's history on the big screen should perhaps not begin their journey with the highly romanticized 2022 biopic *Lamborghini: The Man Behind The Legend*. Originally set to star Antonio Banderas and Alec Baldwin, it arrived after several years 'in turnaround' (to use Hollywood parlance) and featured Frank Grillo as Ferruccio Lamborghini and – very curiously – Irish actor Gabriel Byrne playing Enzo Ferrari in an incongruous hairpiece. Audience and critical reception were tepid at best.

OPPOSITE: An official biography of Ferruccio Lamborghini, written by his son, was recently made into a film starring Frank Grillo.

ABOVE: Grillo arrived at the Rome Film Festival in a Miura.

The Lamborghini brand was still a young one in 1969 when it made a huge impact – literally – on the general population in the seminal crime caper film *The Italian Job*. For many people this will have been the first sight-and-sound experience of the Miura, hustling and bellowing through the foothills of the snow-capped Colle de Gran San Bernardo with heist mastermind Roger Beckerman at the wheel, a cigarette jauntily hanging out of his mouth. The sequence lasts almost precisely three minutes, the V12 chatter fading in the mix as Matt Munro croons 'On Days Like These' while the credits roll… and then the Miura skids and crashes in a tunnel, to be pulled out by a bulldozer that has been waiting along with a mafia 'welcoming' committee. The burned wreckage is pushed off a cliff edge. Romance and roguery rolled into one exquisitely shot and tightly edited reel.

Not only did this capture the imagination of the cinema-going public, it begat many myths. Enzo Moruzzi, then a junior salesman and demo driver and latterly Lamborghini's head of sales, not only drove the Miura to the location, he was also at the controls for every shot except the in-car footage of actor Rossano Brazzi. Moruzzi's orders were simply to bring the car back undamaged, especially the white leather upholstery (Moruzzi sensibly had the seats swapped out for black equivalents, leaving only the head restraints white). For half a century the precise identity of the Miura used in filming was a mystery and the focus of intense speculation among marque aficionados. It was not destroyed. A second car, already wrecked – accounts differ as to how and where – was used for the post-crash sequence and, it is claimed, had already been removed when the crew went to recover it the next morning.

Since the 'running' Miura was to be delivered to its customer as new, Lamborghini had disconnected the odometer and, once back at Sant'Agata, it was carefully refinished and sent on to a dealer in Rome without a hint of its starring role. Only in 2019 did the company tally up its own records with the research of previous owners, confirming chassis 3568 – currently in the

BELOW: The Miura's brief appearance in *The Italian Job* has ensured it a place in popular culture.

OPPOSITE: While the Countach and its occupants are mere footnotes to the plot, it took centre-stage in the poster for *The Cannonball Run*.

hands of celebrated Liechtenstein car collector Fritz Kaiser – as the star of the film.

'Lesser' Lamborghinis have also appeared on screen as generic Italian exotica. Roger Moore, in his last film before donning James Bond's tuxedo, drove one of only five right-hand-drive Isleros in *The Man Who Haunted Himself*. But for the most part, films and TV series featuring milder Lambos have been relatively obscure themselves, such as 1971's TV film *Mooch Goes To Hollywood* (Islero, 400 GT 2+2), the animated series *Archer* (350 GT), and the peculiar potboiler *Bloodline* (Silhouette) – Audrey Hepburn's only R-rated film, described as "*the worst film of 1979*" by critic Roger Ebert.

It was in the early 1980s that Lamborghini became the go-to brand for on-screen excess, a ruder and less elegant counterpoint to Ferrari in an era characterized by libertarian ostentation. In *The Cannonball Run*, a film whose reliance on lazy gender and racial stereotyping renders it niche viewing in the twenty-first century, spandex-clad Adrienne Barbeau and Tara Buckman race across America in a Countach LP400S, flashing cleavage to distract traffic police. More recently Kanye West based the lyrical hook of his 2012 hit 'Mercy' around the Murciélago; detail-minded R&B fans continue to be vexed by the fact that the car in the video is actually a Gallardo (apparently the only model available on the day of shooting).

As films aspiring to blockbuster status grew bigger, noisier and more expensive, naturally the Murciélago and its relatives were deployed as visual shorthand: a Centenario LP770-4 appears as both a car and an autobot in *Transformers: The Last Knight*, Benedict Cumberbatch's egomaniac *Doctor Strange* drives a Huracán, and Murciélagos and an Aventador have given the custom machinery a run for its money in Christopher Nolan's *Dark Knight* trilogy. There is an amusing exchange in *The Dark Knight* in which butler Alfred asks if Bruce Wayne will be using

Burt Reynolds Roger Moore

Farrah Fawcett Dom DeLuise

Dean Martin Sammy Davis, Jr. Adrienne Barbeau

Jamie Farr Terry Bradshaw Mel Tillis

MAXIMUM SPEED 55

You'll root for them all...
but you'll never guess who wins.

GOLDEN HARVEST PRESENTS AN ALBERT S. RUDDY PRODUCTION · A HAL NEEDHAM FILM "THE CANNONBALL RUN"
Co-Starring JACKIE CHAN · MICHAEL HUI · Executive Producer RAYMOND CHOW · Produced by ALBERT S. RUDDY
Written by BROCK YATES · Directed by HAL NEEDHAM
Music Conducted by AL CAPPS

PG PARENTAL GUIDANCE SUGGESTED
SOME MATERIAL MAY NOT BE SUITABLE FOR CHILDREN

READ THE LEISURE PAPERBACK

810048
"CANNONBALL RUN"

BELOW: Six Huracáns were used in filming *Doctor Strange*, and one was destroyed in the pivotal crash sequence.

ABOVE: One of only 40 Centenarios to be built stars as both car and autobot in *Transformers: The Last Knight.*

the Batpod for an urgent mission; when the response comes back negative he sighs, "*The Lamborghini then. Much more subtle.*"

Perhaps the ultimate alliance of the bull with absurd excess came in *The Wolf of Wall Street*, in which central character Jordan Belfort, the corrupt stockbroker played with gleeful relish by Leonardo Di Caprio, attempts to drive home from his country club in his Lamborghini Countach 25th Anniversary (white, naturally) after a quaalude binge. In his mind the journey unfolds without incident; a flashback sequence depicts the

violently chaotic reality. Cut to the car itself, wheels akimbo and no panel left straight.

Appropriately enough for Lamborghini, a fascinating myth developed around this sequence based on an anonymous trivia submission to the Internet Movie Database: director Martin Scorsese thought a substitute 'kit' car would look inauthentic… so he had the real Countach trashed. Would even this famously exacting film-maker order such a valuable asset to be virtually destroyed? Surely not.

BELOW: 'Lude conduct? Director Martin Scorsese had real 25th Anniversary Countach trashed while filming Jordan Belfort's quaalude binge in *The Wolf of Wall Street*.

In fact, it was. Two very rare US-spec Countachs were used in filming, one rented for second-unit purposes. The other was used for all the stunts and left with authentic damage after each impact. Then, deeming it not looking *quite* bent enough, Scorsese had a flatbed truck drive over it. It was the end of the road for that Countach, with just 11,300km (7,021 miles) on the clock. A decade after the film's release, it was offered for auction by Bonhams in a sale during the 2023 Abu

Dhabi Formula 1 Grand Prix weekend, with authenticating material and various merchandise including a director's chair and clapperboard signed by Scorsese. *"A time capsule of the era's elegant debauchery,"* claimed the catalogue. *"The very vehicle that had you contemplating quitting your day job for a Wall Street escapade!"*

Perhaps embodying the spirit of this age, the car was bid up to $1.35million but failed to meet its reserve of $1.5million.

INDEX

(Key: *italic* refers to photos/captions)

S

T

U

V

W

Z

CREDITS

The publishers would like to thank the following sources for their kind permission to reproduce the pictures in this book:

ALAMY: Dave Adams 36, 37; Album 154-155; Ian Bottle 20-21; Mariusz Burcz 98-99, 109, 114, 118-119; Ivan Caravona 45; Joshua Claro 72; P Cox 102; culture-images GmbH 127; Grzegorz Czapski 101; Mark Fagelson 95; Goddard Archive 64-65, 108; Heritage Image Partnership Ltd 34, 38-39, 70, 84-85; John Heseltine 50; The History Collection 11; Imageplotter News and Sports 147; KL_Neo 106-107; Gennaro Leonardi 146; PictureLux/The Hollywood Archive 149; Sam Rollinson 152-153; TCD/Prod.DB 144, 150-151; WENN Rights Ltd 103; Tom Wood 18; Zuma Press 71

GETTY IMAGES: Simon Dawson/Bloomberg 112; Klemantaski Collection 30-31

MOTORSPORT IMAGES: 15, 25, 28, 53, 54, 55, 56-57, 62, 63, 68, 75, 76, 78T, 78B, 82, 83, 86, 87, 93, 138; Ercole Colombo 128-129; JEP 140; LAT Photographic 8; David Phipps 33; Jamey Price 139; Rainer Schlegelmilch 22-23, 130; Sutton 124, 132-133, 134, 135, 136-137

SHUTTERSTOCK: Lucille Cottin 41; FernandoV 24; Sergey Kohl 19, 48; Magic Car Pics 12; Jarlat Maletych 120-121; MarshyPhotography 80-81; Nolichuckyjake 35; Olycom Spa 16; Paul Pollock 60-61; Scott Sim 59; Jack Skeens 42-43; Sport car hub 4, 100, 104-105; Krivosheev Vitaly 116-117; Brandon Woyshnis 90, 94